DUNG BEETLE VS. TARANTULA HAWK

BY NATHAN SOMMER

BELLWETHER MEDIA • MINNEAPOLIS, MN

TM

Torque brims with excitement
perfect for thrill-seekers of all kinds.
Discover daring survival skills, explore
uncharted worlds, and marvel at mighty
engines and extreme sports. In *Torque* books,
anything can happen. Are you ready?

This edition first published in 2023 by Bellwether Media, Inc.

No part of this publication may be reproduced in whole or in part without written
permission of the publisher. For information regarding permission, write to
Bellwether Media, Inc., Attention: Permissions Department,
6012 Blue Circle Drive, Minnetonka, MN 55343.

Library of Congress Cataloging-in-Publication Data

Names: Sommer, Nathan, author.
Title: Dung beetle vs. tarantula hawk / by Nathan Sommer.
Description: Minneapolis, MN : Bellwether Media, Inc., 2023. | Series:
    Torque. Animal battles | Includes bibliographical references and index.
    | Audience: Ages 7-12 | Audience: Grades 4-6 | Summary: "Amazing
    photography accompanies engaging information about the fighting
    advantages of dung beetles and tarantula hawks. The combination of
    high-interest subject matter and light text is intended for students in
    grades 3 through 7"– Provided by publisher.
Identifiers: LCCN 2022038245 (print) | LCCN 2022038246 (ebook) | ISBN
    9798886871654 (library binding) | ISBN 9798886872132 (paperback) | ISBN
    9798886872910 (ebook)
Subjects: LCSH: Dung beetles–Juvenile literature. | Pepsis–Juvenile
    literature.
Classification: LCC QL596.S3 S67 2023 (print) | LCC QL596.S3 (ebook) |
    DDC 595.76/49–dc23/eng/20220829
LC record available at https://lccn.loc.gov/2022038245
LC ebook record available at https://lccn.loc.gov/2022038246

Editor: Kieran Downs   Designer: Josh Brink

Printed in the United States of America, North Mankato, MN.

TABLE OF CONTENTS

THE COMPETITORS

Millions of **insects** live beneath the earth's surface. Dung beetles break down animal waste to keep the soil healthy. Their strong legs can fight off enemies.

Tarantula hawks have deadly stings.
They can bring down enemies that
are much bigger than themselves.
Who would win if these two insects met?

Dung beetles have round, dark-colored bodies. They are found on every **continent** except Antarctica. The insects live in many **habitats**.

Dung beetles survive using the **feces** of other animals. Many roll dung into large balls that they bury underground. They feed off of it. Many also lay their eggs in it.

OWL FOOD

Owls eat dung beetles. They sometimes use feces as a trap to catch these insects.

DUNG BEETLE PROFILE

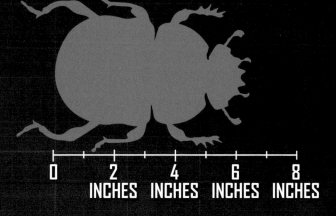

```
0        2        4        6        8
       INCHES   INCHES   INCHES   INCHES
```

LENGTH
UP TO 6.7 INCHES
(17 CENTIMETERS)

WEIGHT
UP TO 3.5 OUNCES
(99 GRAMS)

HABITAT

GRASSLANDS   FARMLANDS   DESERTS   FORESTS

DUNG BEETLE RANGE

▇ RANGE

7

TARANTULA HAWK PROFILE

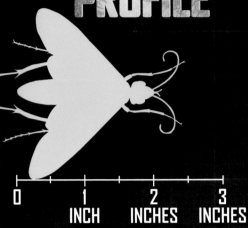

0   1   2   3
INCH INCHES INCHES

LENGTH
UP TO 2 INCHES
(5.1 CENTIMETERS)

WEIGHT
UP TO 0.7 OUNCES
(19.8 GRAMS)

HABITAT

DESERTS   GRASSLANDS   RAIN FORESTS

TARANTULA HAWK RANGE

■ RANGE

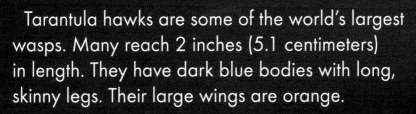

Tarantula hawks are some of the world's largest wasps. Many reach 2 inches (5.1 centimeters) in length. They have dark blue bodies with long, skinny legs. Their large wings are orange.

Tarantula hawks are **solitary**. They live near their favorite **prey**, tarantulas. Females lay eggs in the bodies of their prey.

WARNING COLORS

Tarantula hawks' bright colors warn predators of their painful stings. Attackers know to avoid the insects.

SECRET WEAPONS

Dung beetles have powerful legs.
Their back legs help them move heavy
objects. Some **species** can move things
1,141 times their weight!

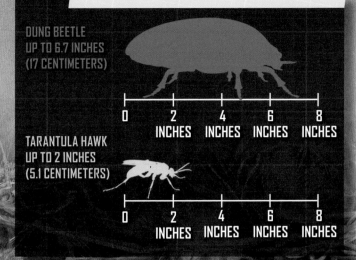

DUNG BEETLE
UP TO 6.7 INCHES
(17 CENTIMETERS)

| 0 | 2 INCHES | 4 INCHES | 6 INCHES | 8 INCHES |

TARANTULA HAWK
UP TO 2 INCHES
(5.1 CENTIMETERS)

| 0 | 2 INCHES | 4 INCHES | 6 INCHES | 8 INCHES |

Female tarantula hawks use stingers for protection and hunting. They have one of the world's most painful stings. One sting is usually enough to scare off most **predators**.

Male dung beetles use their strong horns to protect their dung. They grab and flip other beetles. Some horns are as long as the beetle's bodies!

HORN

Tarantula hawk stings release **venom** into prey. This **paralyzes** most enemies. The wasps use this to take down enemies much larger than themselves.

SECRET WEAPONS

DUNG
BEETLE

**POWERFUL
LEGS**

**STRONG
HORNS**

**STRONG
WINGS**

Dung beetles are excellent fliers. They have two strong pairs of wings. Many can fly for miles at a time without stopping. This helps them escape attackers.

14

SHARP STINGERS   VENOM   HOOKED CLAWS

Tarantula hawks have long legs with hooked claws. Their legs allow them to quickly chase prey. The claws help the wasps hold on to their prey!

ATTACK MOVES

Dung beetles battle to **defend** their dung! They use their horns to block their underground tunnels. If this fails, they shove enemies with their front legs.

Female tarantula hawks fly near the ground in search of prey. They fly under prey or flip them on their backs. Then they attack!

ONE LONG MEAL

Tarantula hawk prey is often kept alive while being eaten. It may be alive for weeks as it is eaten by tarantula hawk young!

Dung beetles use their strong legs to throw enemies onto their backs. This makes the enemies **defenseless** for a short time. They use strong wings to fly away from losing battles.

FLY CONTROLLERS

Dung beetles were brought to Australia to help the country's fly problem. This is because they eat the feces flies are attracted to!

Tarantula hawks attack enemies with sharp stings. The wasps lay eggs on their paralyzed prey. Then they drag their prey into their **burrows**.

READY, FIGHT!

A dung beetle and a tarantula hawk meet underground. The startled dung beetle flips the tarantula hawk with its horns. Then it runs above ground!

The dung beetle spreads its wings to escape. But the tarantula hawk attacks before the beetle takes off. It grabs and stings the dung beetle. The tarantula hawk found food for its young today!

GLOSSARY

burrows—tunnels or holes in the ground used as animal homes

continent—one of the seven great divisions of land found on the globe

defend—to protect

defenseless—unable to fight back

feces—animal waste

habitats—the homes or areas where animals prefer to live

insects—small animals with six legs and hard outer bodies; an insect's body is divided into three parts.

paralyzes—makes something unable to move

predators—animals that hunt other animals for food

prey—animals that are hunted by other animals for food

solitary—related to living alone

species—kinds of animals

venom—a kind of poison used to hurt or paralyze enemies

TO LEARN MORE

AT THE LIBRARY

Adamson, Thomas K. *Scorpion vs. Tarantula*. Minneapolis, Minn.: Bellwether Media, 2021.

London, Martha. *Beetles*. Minneapolis, Minn.: Pop!, 2020.

McAneney, Caitie. *This Book Stings!* New York, N.Y.: Gareth Stevens, 2020.

ON THE WEB

FACTSURFER

Factsurfer.com gives you a safe, fun way to find more information.

1. Go to www.factsurfer.com

2. Enter "dung beetle vs. tarantula hawk" into the search box and click 🔍.

3. Select your book cover to see a list of related content.

INDEX

The images in this book are reproduced through the courtesy of: cynoclub, cover (dung beetle); Alejandro Santillana/ Flickr, cover (tarantula hawk); IanRedding, pp. 2-3, 20-21, 22-23, 24; Lokibaho/ Getty Images, pp. 2-3, 15 (sharp stingers), 20-21, 22-23, 24; Cristian Gusa, p. 4; Richard Stephen/ Getty Images, p. 5; Hein Myers Photography, pp. 6-7; Steve. Trewhella/ Alamy Stock Photo, pp. 8-9; Rudmer Zwerver/ Alamy Stock Photo, p. 10; Mark Moffett/ Minden, p. 11; Acting Sub Lt.niwat Thumma/ EyeEm/ Getty Images, p. 12; Tonia Graves/ Alamy Stock Photo, p. 13; Nadine Klose, p. 14 (bottom beetle); Dennis van de Water, p. 14 (powerful legs, strong wings); ozgur kerem bulur, p. 14 (strong horns); Rick & Nora Bowers/ Alamy Stock Photo, p. 15 (bottom tarantula hawk); JoniAnne, p. 15 (venom); Vinicius R. Souza, p. 15 (hooked claws); Michael Potter11, p. 16; Tom Wurl, p. 17; Monique Berger/ Biosphoto/ Alamy Stock Photo, p. 18; Phipps_Photography, p. 19.